#50-97   BK Bud   4/97

CHILD LURES

CHILD LURES

What Every Parent and Child Should Know About Preventing Sexual Abuse and Abduction

by

KENNETH WOODEN

THE SUMMIT PUBLISHING GROUP • ARLINGTON, TEXAS

THE SUMMIT PUBLISHING GROUP
One Arlington Centre • 1112 E. Copeland Rd., Fifth Floor
Arlington, Texas 76011

Printed in the United States of America

95 96 97 98 99   5 4 3 2 1

Library of Congress Cataloging-in-Publication Data

Wooden, Kenneth.
    Child lures : what every parent and child should know about preventing sexual abuse and abduction / by Kenneth Wooden
    p. cm.
    ISBN 1-56530-175-7 (hc : alk. paper)
    1. Child sexual abuse. 2. Child sexual abuse—Prevention. 3. Kidnapping—Prevention. I. Title.
HV6570.W66 1995
613.6—dc20

95-2885
CIP

Book design by David Sims
Illustrated by Christi Baughman

To all children:
May you grow and bloom in the warmth of safety,
nurtured with love, laughter, and respect.

■

Contents

Acknowledgments

This effort would have been impossible without the assistance and persistence of five individuals. Len Oszustowicz of The Summit Group spent months tracking me down, and he has my complete admiration for his determination to make this book a reality. I also owe a debt of gratitude to editor Mike Towle for his hard work and never-ending enthusiasm. Three other individuals had equal resolve and invaluable input: Rosemary Wooden, Jennifer Wooden, and John Wooden. Though they are my daughters and son, they are also my colleagues whose professional writing, rewriting, editing, and criticism made the final product a source of pride and, I hope, excellence for parents, present and future.

Special acknowledgment goes to my wife of thirty-seven years, Martha Braun Wooden. When I first came up with the idea to conduct interviews with convicted criminals who prey on children, George Gallup, Jr., of the Gallup Poll offered to set up meetings in the White House and the Justice Department. By meeting with senior members of the Carter and Reagan administrations, I hoped to obtain federal funding to research the lures used by pedophiles. When bureaucrats within both the White House and the Justice Department rejected my plan as a "lousy idea," my wife told me, "If Washington, D.C., thinks it's a lousy idea, it must be brilliant." Without Martha's encouragement, *Child Lures* would still be in the conceptual stage.

A word of thanks to my eldest daughter, Grace Theresa Gilbert, who took time out from full-time work, school, and parenting to review the manuscript. One last thank-you to my granddaughters, Meghann and Sarah, who provided their ten and a half years, and nine years of respective experience to help give this book a youthful viewpoint and make it meaningful to both children and parents.

KEN WOODEN
Shelburne, Vermont

Opening Statement

Dear Parents,

If you have opened this book, you are determined to keep your child safe. So am I.

Child molestation and criminal abduction are among every parent's worst fears. Sadly, there is no question that molestation is a monumental problem in America today. The fact is that as many as 20 percent of girls and 7 percent of boys will experience some type of sexual abuse by age eighteen. As far as kidnapping goes, the most recent estimates point to two hundred to three hundred stranger abductions across America each year. That's an average of at least four children per state annually!

Fortunately, we can take heart in knowing that while child molestation and criminal abduction are the most common crimes against children today, they are also among the most preventable crimes against children. In the pages that follow, you will learn how to protect your child with practical and effective prevention strategies. When you are done, there should be no need for expensive safety gimmicks like emergency beepers or homing beacon tooth implants, because "lure-proofed" youngsters are street-smart youngsters.

I have spent fifteen years crisscrossing America teaching the information in this book to more than two hundred fifty thousand children. Youngsters from a rainbow of backgrounds, as well as their parents and teachers, have embraced Child Lures. A Charlotte, North Carolina, boy's reaction says it all: "I had a lot of fun while I learned something that could save my life. It was an hour of learning that will last a lifetime."

Of course, no one book or program can 100 percent guarantee that your child will elude sexual molestation or criminal abduction. However, children who learn the concepts and prevention strategies in this book are far less likely to fall victim to these crimes. Remember, the vast majority of people would never dream of molesting a child; most people share your concern and desire to protect children.

Several years ago, the National Weather Service reported that tornado-caused deaths had declined by two-thirds between the years 1987 and 1988. The reason? Increased public awareness and preparedness. Using this same combination of awareness and prevention, we can and will protect the innocence and lives of children.

Ken Wooden
March 1995

How to Use This Book

It should be obvious from the feel and overall layout of this book, with all its colorful illustrations and explanatory text, that this is a book that should work as an interactive device between parents and their children. Parents or guardians are highly encouraged to read this book first, then sit down with their children and go through it together.

Note that the book consists of three major sections:

- **an introductory section** to be read by parents and guardians;
- **five introductory concepts** that prepare children for understanding the lures; and
- **the main section** of the book, consisting of fifteen mini-chapters—one for each lure—to be read together by the parents and the children.

The first part is primarily for parental use as a background text, while the second and third sections make for excellent reading by parents and children together. Sections of text specific to the child are easy to spot: They are shaded. Children are encouraged to read these shaded sections to themselves and then aloud to their parents.

Each of the fifteen lures' mini-chapters begins with a full-page, color illustration depicting a typical scenario, followed by three subsections:

- **parental text** that contains added background specific to that particular lure;

- **a prevention section** addressed mainly to the child and to be read aloud by the child (the child's reading portion is shaded to set it apart from the rest of the text); and
- **practice scenarios**, with questions to be asked aloud of the child and correct answers that should be reviewed by the child.

It is one thing for parents and guardians to comprehend all that there is to know about child lures and pedophiles; it is another for children to take part in this kind of interactive learning, which could be the difference between safety and tragedy. You love your child/children. Show it by sharing this book with them, preferably one lure at a time.

Profile of the Molester

IN 1986, a United States Customs sting operation, code-named Operation Borderline, culminated in the arrests of one hundred fifty men in thirty-eight states for possession and distribution of child pornography. Prior to the arrests, the majority of these men led seemingly normal lives; some were pillars of the community. Few of us would ever have suspected a secret obsession with child pornography.

The most striking of Operation Borderline's findings was the lack of a tidy criminal profile. The offenders came from all walks of life—some were married, some single, some professional, some blue-collar, some young, some retired. All told, eighty-eight different occupations were represented, including attorney, farmer, policeman, bartender, dentist, machinist, auditor, electrician, school bus driver, engineer, and so on. Some preferred boys, and some preferred girls. Some were attracted to young children, others to older children. Pedophilia, or sexual attraction to children by an adult, is a sickness nondiscriminating against race, class, or age. It knows no bounds, and those pedophiles infiltrate every segment of society.

Several years before Operation Borderline, I committed to learning more about pedophiles and how they secure their victims. I had recently left my position as investigative reporter and field producer for two television news magazines, so I was eager to help prevent the same horrors I had reported. The next few years I visited prisons and psychiatric hospitals across the country, interviewing convicted sex offenders who preyed on children. What I learned from those hundreds of incarcerated pedophiles, some of them murderers, is the heart of this book.

Pedophiles, try as they might, are unable to resist the powerful urge to initiate sexual contact with children. As a result, molesters often make efforts to gain access to—or authority over—children. They take jobs where children are easily approached, or they actively pursue youngsters by befriending single parents, attending events for children, coaching children's sports, chaperoning camping trips, frequenting video arcades, or offering baby-sitting services to friends, family, and neighbors with children. The majority of pedophiles prefer children on the brink of puberty and prey on a child's sexual ignorance and curiosity. One molester told me, "Give me a kid who knows nothing about sex, and you've given me my next victim."

The overwhelming majority of pedophiles are male; the very small percentage of women who do abuse children sexually are usually cooperating with a male aggressor. It is for this reason I refer to pedophiles as "he" throughout this text.

Pedophile Organizations

Small groups of militant and highly organized child molesters operate worldwide through pedophile organizations, whose members claim genuine concern for the welfare of children. Their belief is that sex with children is harmless; some even claim that sexual relations are healthy for children. These groups' goals include decriminalizing child molestation and lowering the age of consent.

The actual number of members in these organizations is unknown, though one, the Rene Guyon Society, is listed in the *Gale Encyclopedia of Associations* as having five thousand members. Other major pedophile organizations include The North American Man-Boy Love Association (NAMBLA) and Pedophile Alert Network (PAN) of the Netherlands. Members receive monthly magazines and newsletters that include seduction techniques and advice on avoiding detection or prosecution. One group's "Lure of the Month" column gives advice on approaching and seducing children. In one month's column, soap crayons were praised for their effectiveness: "children undress themselves!"

NAMBLA's "Entrapment of the Month" column has alerted members to covert government child-pornography sting operations. In one newsletter alone, NAMBLA correctly identified ten sting operations in five different states. In just three years, NAMBLA exposed and compromised four federal sting operations as well, including: Project Looking Glass, Candy's Love Club, Project Sea Hawk, and Project Borderline. Clearly, these organizations have connections.

In addition to attending pedophile conferences and conventions, some child molesters meet via the internet or on-line computer services, where they have been known to swap names, descriptions, and even photographs of molested children. Customs officials indicate that communication via computer is quickly replacing the printed pedophile newsletter.

Remember, the average child molester does not belong to a pedophile organization. However, we would be foolish not to take seriously any group whose members are committed to sexual activity with children.

The Incest Dilemma

During the course of my interviews with pedophiles, I was most disturbed by those who had violated the dignity of family members. Statistics indicate that half of all sexual abuse is incestuous in nature. But it's important to acknowledge the good news: The overwhelming majority of children live in homes free of sexual abuse and are, thankfully, ignorant of such crimes. Preserving that innocence is my priority; to do otherwise, I feel, is an insult to incest-free families. By teaching children that boundaries exist that no adult may cross, it becomes unnecessary to dwell on incest.

The issue of incest is touchy in the best of families. Fathers have told me, "I'm afraid to hug my daughter for fear of being accused of sexual abuse." To those fathers I say, sincere love is the paramount family bond and must not be undermined by the criminal acts of some. Though I have borne witness to the worst of human behavior, including unspeakable crimes against children, I hold with each passing day a stronger conviction that most people are virtuous and intent on safeguarding the innocence of childhood.

You, the parent, must reinforce this point. Don't scare your children beyond the realities of life. It is important to remember that where the media is concerned, only bad news makes good news. For every crime reported, there are literally hundreds of good deeds going unreported. Don't let the media's daily dose of bad news cloud your world view. Those who commit crimes against children are few in number compared to the millions of caring parents in this country. Keep your perspective.

The Stranger

Nearly every parent has told his or her child, "Don't talk to strangers." While it is well-meaning advice, I'm sorry to tell you that it very rarely protects children from sexual assault and abduction.

Most children aren't at all clear as to what constitutes a "stranger." When asked to draw or describe a stranger, many youngsters will invoke frightening and menacing images. The fact is, the typical molester is notoriously personable with youngsters and will go out of his way to dispel any fears a child might have. In the eyes of a child, even a complete stranger who engages a youngster in friendly conversation quickly becomes someone that child "knows." What's more important, most children suffer abuse at the hands of someone they do know, not a complete stranger.

We can't possibly be with our children every waking moment, so it is essential that we provide them with the knowledge to protect themselves. While the proverbial stranger can still pose a threat to the safety of children, we owe it to our kids to teach them much more than the "don't talk to strangers" mantra.

Abduction

• •

To most people, the word "abduction" conjures up images of children kidnapped, raped, and killed by a complete stranger. More often, children are abducted by someone they know, detained for a short period of time, abused, and then released. While "only" two to three hundred children are kidnapped by strangers each year, those numbers fail to reflect the scores of youngsters whose abductions are not necessarily by strangers and do not conclude in death.

The Fear Factor

• •

We all hope to preserve the innocence of our children for as long as possible. Still, so many parents shy away from teaching their children about molestation and abduction, fearing they will frighten children unnecessarily. Left unprepared and vulnerable, generations of abused children now stand as a legacy to that course of inaction.

Remember, even very young children know that some things can be dangerous: moving cars, hot kitchen stoves, electrical outlets, swimming pools, and so forth. Just as we routinely instill in our children a healthy awareness of dangerous things like moving cars, we can also teach them to protect themselves from dangerous people. Keep in mind that most kids today are well aware that sexual abuse, abduction, and even murder can happen to children. You might be surprised how well-informed your children already are.

Children nearly always feel safer after learning prevention strategies. Preventive education turns kids into confident, critical thinkers, prepared for dangerous situations should they arise.

Coaching Pedophiles?

Shortly after I began writing this book, I was asked, "Won't pedophiles be able to use your book as a resource? Won't you give them ideas?" To be honest, I suspect some might borrow these strategies, and I find that thought very disturbing. However, I truly believe that such cases will prove rare. The benefits of disseminating this information far outweigh any negative consequences. Child molesters have cultivated these lures for generations; chances are, they won't learn anything new. They have their own resources. In Austin, Texas, a pedophile used a public-school computer to write the detailed and graphic manual *How to Have Sex with Kids*, which was then made available through underground bookstores across the country.

By compiling pedophiles' "tricks of the trade," my intention is to empower children with the knowledge they need to protect themselves. It is my hope that as more youngsters are "lure-proofed," fewer and fewer pedophiles will succeed in robbing America's children of the priceless innocence of childhood.

In the pages that follow, expect straight talk, conveying vital information to you and your children, in a balanced, non-frightening manner. I've taught thousands of kids all across America how to stay safe. This book will help you do the same for your children.

Introductory Concepts

While numerically and creatively infinite, the lures used by child molesters and abductors generally fall into the following categories:

- Affection
- Assistance
- Authority
- Bribery
- Ego/Fame
- Emergency
- Fun and Games
- Heroes
- Jobs
- Name Recognition
- Playmate
- Threats and Weapons
- Pornography
- Drugs
- Computer/On-line

Keep in mind that children learn best through repetition; your child needs to hear this information more than once. And look for ways to reinforce these concepts and lessons during the course of everyday life. Remember, kids are incredibly bright. They catch on fast.

Before teaching the lures and prevention strategies to young children, I recommend covering the following five concepts with your child:

- People Are Like the Weather
- What Is a Lure?
- You and Your Instincts
- Rules and Laws
- Dignity

PEOPLE ARE LIKE THE WEATHER

Most adults are good people. They are kind and make every effort to keep you safe and happy. Then again, there are some adults out in the world who aren't quite so nice. People are like the weather: Sometimes it's good and safe, and sometimes it's bad and not so safe.

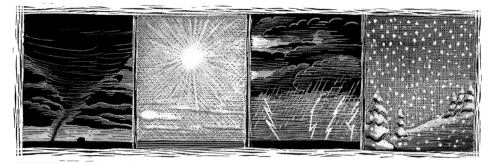

Let's think about the weather a little bit. What kinds of weather can you think of? Warm, sunny days. Winter snowfall. Heavy rains. Tornadoes and hurricanes. What kind of weather is most common where you live? By now, you know how quickly the weather can change. A warm, sunny day can suddenly become stormy, with rain and lightning.

People are like the weather: They can change, sometimes without warning. Most people are nice and safe, but a nice person can quickly become a not-so-nice person. Sometimes people who seem nice do bad things.

Ask yourself:

- "Would I go outside and play during a tornado?"

- "Should we drive during a blizzard?"
- "Would my family go on a picnic during a hurricane?"

Of course, the smart answer to each of those questions is "no." Tornadoes, blizzards, and hurricanes all are dangerous weather conditions. You stay out of danger by protecting yourself from bad weather. The same is true about protecting yourself from "bad-weather people." That's what this book is all about.

WHAT IS A LURE?

Have you ever gone fishing? Do you like to fish? Have you ever caught a fish? If you haven't gone fishing yourself, you might know someone who has.

What do you need to catch a fish? You need:

- a line
- a hook
- bait

As you probably know, bait is what goes on the hook at the end of the line. It gets the fish's attention so that it will bite your hook. Another word for bait is "lure." Just what does a lure do? It brings the fish to the hook, which the fish bites, and then the fish is reeled in. The same thing can happen with people—you, if you're not careful.

There are people out there who, like fishermen going after fish, will try to catch children with lures. The idea is to trick or force a child into going with someone or doing something. These criminals will try to "lure" you in one of many ways. They might promise you a gift, ask you for help, tell you there is an emergency, or even threaten you. They use these methods to get you to go willingly or to get you to do something you really don't want to do. You and your parents need to be able to recognize these lures when you see or hear them. Then, you have to be ready to take action and protect yourself.

Ask yourself:

- "Does my school have fire drills?"
- "How often does my school have fire drills?"
- "Has there ever actually been a fire at school where someone was hurt?"
- "Do I feel safer knowing what to do in case there is a fire at school?"

Learning about lures is a lot like having a fire drill at school. You need to know what to do—just in case.

YOU AND YOUR INSTINCTS

What are "instincts"? Instincts are feelings inside of you that tell you things. Sometimes instincts tell you that things are wrong or even dangerous. These types of instincts can be compared to the siren on a fire truck, police car, or ambulance. What does a siren tell you? It tells you that something is wrong, someone has been hurt, or someone is in danger.

How does hearing a siren make you feel? Excited? Worried? A little frightened? Maybe all of those things at the same time. Point to where those feelings come from. You probably pointed to your stomach, which some people also call their "gut." Some people refer to an instinct as a "gut feeling." Now you know where that phrase comes from.

Your instincts are your own personal siren telling you to "slow down," or "proceed with caution."

Ask yourself:
- "Have I ever met someone who made me feel uneasy, a person I would describe as 'weird'?"

■ "Have I ever had a funny feeling about a person or situation, but c o u l d n ' t explain why?"

Instincts are what make you feel that way. They are the body's way of telling you to be careful. You have been blessed with a great inner siren called "instincts" to help guide you through life. You might not be able to explain them or even understand them all the time. But they are there, protecting you. If you recognize, trust, and follow your instincts, they will be a big help in keeping you safe. Every time you hear a siren, remind yourself about this idea of your own personal siren and listen to it—always.

RULES AND LAWS

Do you have rules you must follow at home? At school? Of course you do. What happens when you break those rules? You get punished, don't you? Well, rules aren't made only

for children. Adults have rules they must follow, too. Those rules are called laws. Laws are a set of rules made to protect people just like you. Laws are made by governments and are expected to be followed by everyone. When adults break the law, they usually get punished.

One law says that adults are not to touch children's private parts—those parts of your body covered by a bathing suit. Those parts are "private" parts because they are yours and no one else's. Your body is *your* private property. It belongs only to you. It's against the law for anyone to touch the private parts of your body or force you to touch theirs.

However, there *are* times when a person might need to see or touch your private parts. Some of those times include visits to the doctor (at least one of your parents should go with you), during bath time at home, or when a baby's diapers are to be changed.

There is a name for an adult who wrongly touches your private parts: That person is called a "molester."

TIP: A molester can be anybody: a neighbor, a relative, the bus driver, a complete stranger, or even a playmate. If anyone touches or attempts to touch your private parts, tell your parents or another trusted adult *immediately*. It's also important to tell the police. Molestation is against the law, and molesters know it is against the law. Reporting abuse might protect other kids, maybe even your friends, from molestation.

If someone touches or tries to touch your private parts, don't be afraid or embarrassed to tell your parents. You are not to be embarrassed for reporting this. Instead, you are to be commended! Your parents need to know this so they can help you.

Remember, discussing problems with a caring adult will almost always make you feel better. Don't be afraid to talk about it, even if the person who touched you is someone you don't want to tell on. This is one time you really need to tell. If for some reason the person you tell can't help, tell another trusted grown-up. Keep telling until someone helps you and the abuse stops.

PARENTS: Your child might be embarrassed or afraid to talk about what happened. The abuser might be someone he knows who he doesn't want to get in trouble. The child might have been threatened into silence. Explain to your child that people who molest children are criminals who should be punished. Only by reporting the crime can the abuse be stopped.

While I strongly encourage children to report abuse, it would be irresponsible of me not to address the issue of false accusations. Although rare, these types of allegations can have serious and far-reaching ramifications.

Also remember that it is against the law to say someone did something wrong when they did not.

Ask yourself:
- "Did a sister, brother, or friend of mine ever say I did something wrong— and I didn't—but I was punished anyway?" (Maybe you have several examples.)

How did that make you feel? Not so great, right? Was that fair? No. Would it be fair to say someone abused you when they did not? Of course not.

TIP: Don't make up stories about abuse. Always tell the truth.

PARENTS: It is important that you explain the seriousness of falsely accusing someone of sexual abuse. Explain how that person could go to jail, lose his family, or lose his job. Tell your child it's against the law to accuse someone of a crime they did not commit. But make sure you don't discourage a child from reporting the real thing.

DIGNITY

You are a young person, but you are an important person, as important as any grown-up. Many people love you and care about you. They need you and you need them. You are a person who deserves to be treated with respect and dignity. Anyone who says you don't is not telling the truth.

13

Now, take some time to think about yourself. What are those things you like about yourself? What are some things about yourself you would like to improve? Be honest. Everything about you—both the things you like and the things you aren't crazy about—makes you a one-of-a-kind person. You are unique and special; there is no one else in the entire world just like you.

I think you will agree that you are pretty special and deserve to be treated well by others. Do you know the word "dignity"? Dignity means "worth." You should expect people to treat you with respect and dignity, *because you're worth it!* This doesn't mean that you're *better* than other people, only that you are as valuable as they are.

Ask yourself:

■ "If someone touches the private parts of my body or asks me to touch his, is that treating me with respect and dignity?"

No. Think of people as snowflakes: No two are alike. Each one of us is different and beautiful in our own way. And each one of us deserves to be treated—and should treat each other—with respect and dignity.

PARENTS: By nurturing a sense of self-worth, we can instill in children the expectation to be treated with respect and dignity.

It is very important that you know the difference between "real love" and "fake love."

The Affection Lure

1

In Fort Smith, Arkansas, a local child molester revealed that one of his victims, after participating in a Girl Scout safety program, told him, "I'm glad I'm not being sexually abused." Since the sexual abuse she suffered at his hands was not outright painful, in her mind it wasn't abuse.

The Affection Lure is the most insidious of all child lures—it exploits the unfulfilled emotional needs of children. This common lure is difficult to recognize and prevent, since it usually escalates slowly from seemingly innocent behavior into full-blown abuse. Sadly, the abuser caters to the most basic of human needs.

Molesters I interviewed disclosed that children starved for affection or attention are among the easiest to befriend and seduce. Other easy targets include youngsters from unhappy family situations, those lacking a male or female role model, or children whose parents are in the middle of a bitter divorce. Pedophiles are also adept at exploiting the normal tensions between children—especially young teenagers—and parents. Some years ago, a mother shared with me the following "Letter From a Molester."

Dear Parents,

I am a pedophile. That's child molester to the layman. I am writing to you to let you know I will soon be molesting your child. Oh, you don't think so? Well, let me tell you how easy it is.

When you don't listen to what your child has to say and regard it as unimportant, childish chatter, you're sending your child to me. I have ears to hear all he/she has to say.

When you scold your child or belittle your little child in front of his/her friends, you're sending your child to me. I can dry his/her tears.

When you don't cuddle your child on your lap or give him/her hugs, you are sending your child to me. My lap is big enough to hold any child, and I have an endless amount of hugs.

When you don't give your child praise, you're sending your child to me. I have an ample supply of attention and affection to give.

Who am I, you ask? I could be your next-door neighbor, a co-worker, a child's teacher, a scout leader. You could know me and you may not know me, but your child knows me.

I am that nice man who is giving your child all that attention and affection you denied him or her. In return, all your child has to do is comply with my sexual wishes. I cannot be stopped, either.

Your pride that your child could not be molested, your unconcern that your neighbor's child might be molested, your ignorance about how I operate, and your lack of interest to find out makes it so easy for me and others like me to prey on your children.

I think you'll agree that this message speaks volumes. Take note and refer back to it often.

. . . .

PREVENTION

CHILDREN: When grown-ups pay attention to you or do things with you, it is usually because they really care about you. They were boys and girls at one time, just like you, and they know how important it is for adults to care about you. Almost all of the time, this adult care and attention is real. They would not do anything to hurt you.

It is very important that you know the difference between "Real Love" and "Fake Love." Real Love is when Mom or Dad tucks you into bed at night. It could also be your grandparents hugging you, or your brother or sister letting you play with his or her toys.

But you should also be on the lookout for Fake Love. This might be when someone, even someone you love or know very well, asks to touch your private parts or asks you to touch his. Or they will touch your private parts without asking you. This is wrong! What are private parts? Those are the parts of your body covered by your bathing suit. Remember, you should always be treated with respect. It is *not* respect when someone touches your private parts.

TIP: If an adult or older child tries to touch the private parts of your body, do the following things:
- **Tell the person(s) to stop.**
- **Leave immediately. If that person won't let you go, scream for help.**
- **Tell a trusted adult, usually your parent, what happened. Your parents should then report this abuse or attempted abuse to police.**

PARENTS: It's important to use the terms "Real Love" and "Fake Love" versus "Good Touch" and "Bad Touch," since a bad touch can actually feel good.

Question the motives of adults who spend a lot of time alone with your child, especially overnight. Rely heavily on parental instincts. Monitor activities in youth groups, at summer camp, and after school. Personally partic-

ipate in these activities or drop by unannounced from time to time. Remember: Report such abuse or attempted abuse to police.

. . . .

PRACTICE SCENARIOS

Anna's parents are divorced. Anna lives with her mother, and her father lives in another part of the country. One day her father calls and tells her he can't wait to have her come visit. Can she come next month? What should Anna do?

Anna is lucky to be able to visit her dad when he lives so far away. Anna and her mom should sit down and plan the visit together.

Shauna really likes her new stepfather, but one night, he comes into her room while she is asleep and tries to get into bed with her. What should Shauna do?

Shauna should be assertive. She should tell her stepfather to sleep in his own bed, then she should tell her mother or another trusted adult. Shauna should scream for help if he will not leave, or if he tries to touch her.

*It is okay to refuse to help someone
who makes you feel uneasy in any way.*

The Assistance Lure

2

In Chattanooga, Tennessee, an eleven-year-old girl was asked directions to a nearby school, which she gave. Minutes later, the man returned to thank her and offered to read her palm. When the young girl held out her hand, he attempted to yank her into the car. The girl broke free and ran to safety.

This compelling lure appeals to the helpful nature of children and is the most popular lure among criminal child abductors. In documented cases, youngsters have been asked for directions, physical assistance, or help looking for a lost pet.

Some molesters/abductors I interviewed spoke of targeting children they spotted while driving. When asked for directions to popular landmarks, fast-food restaurants, or nearby streets, many children will approach a car without hesitation.

Pedophiles are known to prey on children's love for animals, particularly cuddly pets like puppies. In countless cases I've studied, young children are enlisted to help search for a "lost" pet, then lured into a secluded outdoor area or private home where abuse—or worse—can happen.

I've demonstrated the effectiveness of this particular lure with children and young people all over the country. Oprah Winfrey was so taken with the potency of this lure that she asked me to demonstrate it for her viewers. Oprah's producers and I approached several young mothers in a suburban park to ask for their cooperation with our experiment. Each mother emphatically insisted her child would never leave the park with a stranger, then watched in horror from a distance as her youngster cheerfully followed me out of the park to look for my "puppy." On average, it took thirty-five seconds to lure each child away from the safety of the park.

Children might also be approached to help carry packages to a car or into a home. Once inside a building, abuse can occur. Once inside a vehicle, abduction is possible. Some perpetrators even pretend to be in need of a helping hand, in some cases sporting a sling, or serial killer Ted Bundy's favorite, a fake cast.

. . . .

PREVENTION

CHILDREN: You have done many good things. Your parents know this and appreciate it. You also have done nice things for relatives and friends. Maybe it has been household chores, cheering someone up, or helping your brother or sister with homework. You are to be praised for your good works. Helping people makes you feel good, doesn't it?

However, it is okay to refuse to help someone who makes you feel uneasy in any way. Maybe it's an adult in a car asking for directions. Or it could be someone asking you to help find a lost animal. Remember, adults shouldn't be asking you for help. They should be asking other adults to help them. You shouldn't help them by yourself. Politely tell such people you can't help them without first asking your parents.

TIP: If someone in a car stops to ask you directions, take two giant steps away from the car and be prepared to run like the wind in the opposite direction. It is important to stay beyond arm's reach of vehicles.

PARENTS: You can demonstrate this point with your own car. While sitting in the driver's seat, have your child approach the window and show how easy it is for an adult to grab a child who comes too close to a vehicle. Then have your child take two giant steps back from the car: She will see what a big difference a small distance can mean to her safety.

> **TIP: If you are asked to help look for a lost puppy—or any animal—do not speak to that person. Run to your house or a nearby friend's house, and tell a trusted adult you know what has happened.**

PARENTS: Those who use this lure typically approach several children before securing a victim. By reporting this lure, your child might save another.

• •

PRACTICE SCENARIOS

Jack's best friend has a broken arm and asks Jack if he will carry his books home from school. What should Jack do?
Jack should lend a helping hand to his best friend.

A man in a car asks Carla for directions to the post office. What should she do?
Carla should stay a safe distance away from the car. If she chooses to give the man directions, she should take two giant steps back from the car and be ready to run in the opposite direction.

A man who lives two streets down from Sarah asks if she would like to come into his house to help feed his newborn puppies. What should Sarah do?
Sarah should tell the man that she must first ask her parents for permission. If Sarah's parents say that it is all right, she can go. Ideally, one parent should accompany her, especially if they don't know the neighbor.

Authority figures in your life should not ask you to do things that are against the law or make you feel scared.

The Authority Lure

enneth Robert Stanton, the first child molester to appear on the FBI's Most-Wanted List, scoured neighborhoods in the South searching for girls who were home alone. Stanton gained access to the children's homes by flashing a phony badge and claiming to be with the health or water department. Once inside, Stanton swiftly blindfolded and sexually assaulted the young girls. Stanton was apprehended after being featured on the television show, Unsolved Mysteries.

We teach children, rightly so, to respect and obey adults. A child molester can take advantage of that respect and obedience by using his position of authority to intimidate or force youngsters into sexual exploitation.

Children might be too timid to refuse advances from a grownup, or feel they must do whatever an adult tells them to do—be it a teacher, bus driver, coach, parent, neighbor, relative, or baby-sitter.

To aid in abduction of children, some sex criminals go so far as to pose as detectives, police, or truant officers. They might use badges and uniforms or even affix flashing lights or CB radios to a vehicle. These materials can be easily obtained through detective magazines, Army-Navy stores, and law enforcement supply stores.

Custom-made badges are readily available, and serious criminals are well aware of their effectiveness. Youngsters might be approached and accused of a crime, say, shoplifting, then ordered to "Come with me!"

While working as an investigative reporter for ABC News's *20/20*, I obtained a fake badge for $14.95 from a detective magazine. When ABC correspondent Tom Jarriel and I showed it to an FBI agent, the agent remarked it looked more authentic than his own. While working on a special with a Jacksonville TV station, I lured one young man out of a mall by flashing my badge and accusing him of shoplifting. Once outside the mall, the hidden camera crew and I could not help but smile when the boy confided to me in a quavering voice, "Sir, I'm not stealing, but I'll give you the names of four of my friends who are!"

● ●

PREVENTION

CHILDREN: You have many authority figures in your life that you are expected to obey. Authority figures in your life include police officers, your parents, teachers, bus drivers, coaches, relatives, and baby-sitters. You should treat them with respect.

People with authority should not ask you to do things that make you uneasy or that are against the law. You have a right to refuse those types of requests. Don't worry; you won't get into trouble. Your parent will support your decision.

TIP: No adult has the authority to touch your private parts or force you to touch his.

Criminals often use *fake* police badges. They want to trick you into thinking they are someone who can tell you what to do. Question them.

TIP: If you are approached by an adult with a badge, uniform, or official-looking car, and he or she starts asking you questions or speaking to you, tell another adult nearby that you are frightened and that you need help. This will scare off a *fake* authority figure.

Criminals trying to fool you with their *fake* badges like to go after children they see shoplifting, smoking, or hanging out with nothing to do. You should not be stealing or smoking in the first place, for your own good.

PARENTS: Juveniles who are shoplifting, smoking, or loitering are more likely to be intimidated by real or feigned authority. Warn youngsters never to go with a plainclothes officer or get into an unmarked police car. Both are easily simulated. In addition, mall security guards do not have the authority to arrest an individual. They must call police from a mall security office. Teach children to request a uniformed officer and marked car.

Outside a Memphis mall, I showed a nine-year-old boy my fake badge, explained I wanted to talk to him about shoplifting, and told him to get into my car. He didn't budge. When I asked, "Why won't you get in the car?" he looked me in the eye and said, "Because my mama told me not to." He's the only person who ever gave me a flat-out "No!"

Consider visiting your local police department with your child. This will allow him to meet actual police officers and become familiar with local police uniforms, badges, and vehicles.

PRACTICE SCENARIOS

It's Saturday afternoon and Simon is at the mall. A man in a suit approaches, flashes a badge, and asks Simon to step outside to discuss the rash of shoplifting at the mall. What should Simon do?

Under no circumstances should Simon leave the safety of the mall. He should be respectful, but explain that he won't leave the mall with a stranger. Then he should ask for help from a mall employee behind a counter, or ask for a uniformed police officer and marked car. If the man tries to make him leave the mall, Simon should make a commotion and scream if need be.

Alden takes a bus to and from school each day. One day, Alden gets into a loud argument with another boy on the bus. The bus driver tells Alden to move up to the front seat. What should Alden do?

Alden should obey the bus driver and move up to the front seat.

Bribery is when someone gives you something only because they want you to do something for them in return.

The Bribery Lure

4

A retired New Jersey man offered pre-teen boys in his neighborhood the opportunity to tinker with go-carts. Over time, he would initiate sexual contact. Boys who consented to sexual behavior were rewarded with go-carts of their own.

The saying, "Don't take candy from strangers" is dated, but the age-old lure of bribery still works. Young children are offered candy, toys, and money; older children might be tempted with expensive gifts or alcohol and other drugs. Bribes are used to persuade children to go willingly with a molester/abductor, as "payment" for sexual activity, or as a reward for keeping abuse a secret. In my luring demonstrations over the years, I've found the most effective bribe, even for very young children, is money.

For instance, while filming a luring demonstration in Seattle, one little boy proved to be an especially hard sell. I tried to bribe him with candy, toys, and a headset. Each time, he adamantly refused my offer. However, when I offered him a roll of quarters for hours of fun at the local video arcade, his defenses fell, and he took the money.

In some cases, children who are showered with presents and money in exchange for sex allow abuse to continue for a period of time. They agree to keep the activity secret from parents so the gifts will keep coming.

• •

PREVENTION

CHILDREN: For most people, there are several times a year when we give or receive gifts. You probably remember many times when you have given gifts to or received gifts from people you care about.

When was the last time you gave a birthday gift to a brother, sister, friend, or classmate? Another favorite time for gift-giving is during the holiday season. Maybe it's at Christmas or during Hanukkah. It's fun to receive gifts, isn't it? Many people agree it's even more fun to give them. In either case, it is a sincere way for people to show how much they care for each other. That is good.

You should also know that there is another kind of giving, one that isn't so good. This is called bribery. That's when someone gives something to another person and expects something in return. This kind of gift giving—bribery—is wrong. One example would be a criminal trying to give money to a police officer so that the police officer won't arrest the criminal for his bad deed. It could also be someone giving you a gift in return for letting him touch the private parts of your body or having you touch his. This is not right, even if his gift to you is something you like a lot. You know something is wrong if someone gives you a gift and then asks you to keep it a secret.

TIP: If you are asked to keep a gift a secret—even if it's a gift you like or that seems harmless—tell your parents immediately.

Some secrets are okay because they are eventually told, such as keeping your brother's upcoming surprise party a secret. But other secrets can be dangerous, such as if someone touches your private parts and tells you, "This is our special secret."

TIP: A good secret is one that you eventually get to tell. A bad secret is one that makes you feel bad to keep it, or that you are afraid to tell.

PARENTS: Be alert to unexplained toys, gifts, or money. Do your own "IRS Audit." Find out who gave what to your child: when, where, and why.

. . . .

PRACTICE SCENARIOS

Ask your child if she would be tempted by the following:

■ A neighbor offers you an expensive toy if you'll get undressed.

■ A friend's mother offers you a peanut butter and jelly sandwich after school.

■ A man at the playground offers you a headset if you'll leave the school grounds and talk to him.

■ Your teacher offers to let you leave early for recess if you turn in your homework early.

■ A young man offers you a roll of quarters for "lots of fun at the video arcade" if you'll come into his house.

Which offers are appropriate and which could be lures? Which does your child find most tempting?

You should never remove clothing for pictures or video.

The Ego/Fame Lure

leven-year-old Alison Parrott, a Toronto track star, was excited when a man claiming to be a photographer with the local paper called, requesting a photo session. She excitedly called her mother who gave Alison permission to meet the reporter at Varsity Stadium. Alison's lifeless body was found in a park two days later; she had been sexually assaulted and strangled.

Sex criminals might use compliments and offers of fame and fortune to lure children into abuse or abduction. The glamorous life of a model, rock star, professional athlete, or movie star can be extremely attractive to many people, especially young people. Children are easily swayed by the promise of a modeling job, a spot in a talent or beauty contest, or the chance to star in a commercial. Older students might be enticed by fraudulent offers of athletic scholarships or sport contracts.

A perpetrator might initially overwhelm the child with compliments on looks, talent, or personality, then convince him to come along to an immediate audition, or keep a private audition a secret from parents. Youngsters blinded by stars in their eyes might willingly go with the person or agree to meet him at a later date.

The Ego Lure can also be used as a vehicle to engage children in pornographic photos or videos. Illegitimate photo and filming sessions might begin harmlessly, then escalate into seduction or pornography.

· ·

PREVENTION

CHILDREN: There are probably several things in life you are very good at doing. Maybe it's sports, ballet, art, or music. At school, it could be math, science, art, English or history. Ask your parents to help you come up with a list of activities or skills for which you have a talent. Your parents are proud of what you can do and have probably given you a lot of compliments. Well done!

PARENTS: Praise your child for his abilities and attributes. Now, ask your child how he would feel if someone told him:

- "You would be great in commercials."
- "You look like a model."
- "You have a promising career in music/professional sports."

TIP: If you are ever offered a chance to try out for something such as a TV show or a modeling job, tell that person that he or she must first talk to your parents. A REAL talent scout will agree and won't hesitate to discuss this with your parents.

As a child, you can not accept such offers or sign contracts. If someone pretending

to be a talent scout tries to make a deal with you, without your parents involved, don't trust that person. Explain that your parents must be with you when making such a deal.

PARENTS: In one sad story, a young Florida boy won a local kite-flying contest; his picture and address were featured in the local newspaper. A man contacted the boy's parents, represented himself as a surfing equipment company's sales rep, and told them their boy would be perfect for surfing competition demos. After meeting with the boy's parents, the man sent them a letter complimenting their home life. A short time later, by fabricating an emergency in the boy's family, he was able to convince the youngster's school to release the boy into his custody. The boy was later found sexually assaulted and murdered. This story emphasizes the importance of confirming the legitimacy of all talent scouts and agents. Make sure you check with two different sources, one being your local

Better Business Bureau. One family's tragedy is a lesson for us all.

Tell your child never to remove clothing for photographs or videos, no matter what the argument. Prepare your child for compliments such as, "There's nothing wrong with the human body; it's beautiful!" by reminding him the private parts of the body are just that: private. Reinforce that it is against the law for an adult to photograph or videotape the private parts of a child's body. Stress that secrets another adult asks your child to keep from parents are dangerous secrets, and should be shared with you immediately.

PRACTICE SCENARIOS

Jeremy's Uncle Sully always has a camera. He takes pictures of Jeremy all the time and gives them to Jeremy's parents, who are very thankful. One day, when Jeremy is alone with Uncle Sully, his uncle says, "Let's do something different today. Let's take some pictures with your clothes off." What should Jeremy do?

Jeremy should listen to his instincts and refuse to let his uncle—or anyone, for that matter—take photographs of him without clothing. He should tell his parents as soon as possible, especially if his uncle tells him not to tell.

While snowboarding, Dean is approached by a man who claims to represent a snowboard company. The man is very impressed with Dean's abilities and says that his company is looking for a young athlete to endorse its products. He gives Dean a business card and asks him to talk it over with his parents. What should Dean do?
If interested, Dean should discuss the offer with his parents, who then check the man's credentials. If everything checks out, they may call the man for an appointment. Dean's parents should be present for all meetings and appearances.

Someone might make up a story about an emergency just to get you to go with them.

The Emergency Lure

hile I was teaching Child Lures in a Midwest elementary school, a resourceful eight-year-old girl told me that once, when she was walking home from school, a man in a car pulled up alongside her. He told her that her mom had fallen very ill and had to be taken to the hospital. "Your mother asked me to bring you to the hospital. Quickly! Get in the car!" Instead, the little girl ran all the way home. When she burst into the kitchen, there was her mother, safe and sound, cooking dinner.

The Emergency Lure is designed to worry and confuse a child; the very nature of emergencies means quick, impulsive action. By concocting a crisis, perpetrators persuade victims to accompany them without a second thought, instinct overridden by panic. Few adults think clearly when news of tragedy strikes close to home; imagine how worried and frightened a child feels. Some examples of the Emergency Lure follow:

- "Your dad had a heart attack. Your mother sent me to take you straight to the hospital."
- "Your house is on fire and your mother told me to come get you."
- "Your mother was in a car accident and has been taken to the hospital—quick, come with me!"

The child becomes so upset at the prospect of such a crisis, he is easily convinced to go with the perpetrator.

PREVENTION

CHILDREN: You know that there are emergencies in life—things such as floods, fires, and injuries. When was the last time there was an emergency in your family? What was it? How was it handled?

Emergencies are a part of life and will occur from time to time. They usually are totally unexpected. However, don't assume that an emergency is happening just because someone tells you so. Sometimes, people will make up a story about an emergency just to scare you and get you to go away with them, where they might try to hurt you.

TIP: Never go away with someone telling you something like, "Your house is on fire and your dad told me to come get you," or "Your mother has been hurt in a car accident, come with me." Never go away with such a person—especially a complete stranger—until the emergency has been verified. If someone tells you about such an emergency, run or call home, or go to a trusted adult for help.

TIP: Ask your parents to show you how to dial 9-1-1 or the local emergency telephone number.

PARENTS: Ten years ago, I thought the idea of a family "code word" was a good idea. Theoretically, a child would never go with someone unless they were privy to a previously agreed-upon secret password. However, while teaching the lures to well over a quarter million children, I came to realize how likely children are to disclose secret code words to friendly persons. For the past several years, I instead have encouraged children to work with their families to pre-arrange a specific Family Plan of Action in case of emergencies.

Who would contact your child if there really was an emergency in your family? Whom can the child rely on if you are unavailable during an emergency? A relative? Neighbor? Friend's family? Discuss all these questions with your child and determine a Family Plan of Action understood by all.

....

PRACTICE SCENARIOS

Caroline is at the playground with some friends. A woman runs up to her and says that Caroline's dog was just hit by a car, then offers her a ride to the vet. What should Caroline do? Caroline should not go with the woman under any circumstances. If Caroline does own a dog, she should run or call home to see if her dog really was hit by a car.

Seymour's teacher tells him that his mom was in a minor car accident and had to be taken to the hospital. The teacher tells Seymour that his father is on the way and to wait in the school office. What should Seymour do? Seymour should wait for his father in the school office.

If you are like most other children, you probably love to play games both indoors and out.

The Fun and Games Lure

7

A Dayton man preyed on the large population of children in the trailer park where he lived. The game "hide the quarter" provided him with opportunities for body contact, which quickly escalated into sexual abuse. When he was charged with numerous counts of child molestation, police discovered his diary, revealing the names of more than one hundred fifty children he had abused.

Child molesters might suggest or initiate harmless games to promote sexual contact. Tickling, wrestling, bath time, or other body-contact games might begin innocently, then escalate into fondling and sexual abuse. Since physical contact is normal during these games, children are less likely to be aware that anything out of the ordinary is happening. Under these circumstances, child molesters might even convince children that inappropriate contact was purely unintentional.

Common sense dictates that a child should never allow herself to be tied up or handcuffed during the course of games like Cowboys and Indians, or Cops and Robbers. Once restrained, your child is completely defenseless against abuse or abduction.

• •

PREVENTION

CHILDREN: If you are like most other children your age, you love to play games, both indoor games and outdoor games. What are some of the games you like to play? Some games you can play by yourself. There are other games you can play with your friends or family. Maybe it's kickball, dodgeball, tag, hide and seek, or follow the leader. Most of

41

these games are fun and safe and should be enjoyed.

During some games, we touch the people with whom we are playing. That's okay, as long as the parts of the body being touched are not the private parts.

When playing games, either with adults or other children, none of the other players should ever touch or attempt to touch your privates, which are those body parts covered by your bathing suit. There are dozens of games that typically involve some sort of physical contact, such as basketball, baseball, softball, or football, although there is never a right time for players in those and other games to be touching your private parts on purpose.

TIP: If during the course of any game an adult or another child touches or attempts to touch your privates, demand that person stop!

Then tell a parent or other trusted adult.

PARENTS: Remember, while some children play "doctor," there is usually a vast difference between this type of harmless exploration among peers and unwanted or unsolicited sexual abuse.

Listen to your instincts. Question the intent of adults or older children who seem preoccupied by playing with young children. Make sure that organized sports and lessons are well-supervised, either by yourself or other parents. Impromptu visits are encouraged.

• •

PRACTICE SCENARIOS

Kaitlin notices that lately, when her dad's friend Peter tickles her, he always touches her chest under her shirt. No one seems to notice, but it is making Kaitlin very uncomfortable. What should Kaitlin do?
Kaitlin should immediately tell

her parents. Should Peter try to tickle her again, she should tell him she doesn't like it and for him to stop. And again, she should tell her parents.

A neighbor invites Mario to join a family softball game in the park down the street. What should Mario do?
If he would like to play softball, Mario should ask his parents for permission, let them know where he will be, when he will be home, and enjoy the game!

Mr. Jones, a family friend, comes over for dinner. While Jodi's parents get dinner ready, Mr. Jones pulls a quarter from his pocket and asks Jodi to play "Hide the Quarter." First, he hides the quarter under his watch-band, where Jodi finds it. Next, Jodi hides the quarter on her head and Mr. Jones finds it. Finally, Jodi sees Mr. Jones hide the quarter in his pants' pocket. What should she do?
Jodi should stop playing the game. Mr. Jones's pants' pocket is too close to his private parts.

Who are your heroes? Who do you really look up to?

The Hero Lure

8

A $7.4 million settlement was reached against a Redmond, Washington, high school basketball coach convicted of molesting several youths, ranging in age from ten to fifteen. In an emotional statement, the judge in the case said he hoped the substantial settlement would help people understand how devastating sexual abuse can be for children and their families.

Young people seek and cherish the attention of individuals they know and admire. Their heroes might include local celebrities, favorite teachers, parents, and relatives. Some molesters set out to become heroes in the victim's estimation, then take advantage of their position to facilitate molestation or abduction. In cases where the child and abuser know each other, the child might endure repeated abuse to maintain the "friendship," or keep his hero out of trouble.

In far less common cases, individuals pose as famous celebrities—or claim to know them personally—to gain advantage. Very young children have even been abused by molesters dressed as child celebrities, holiday figures, or costumed characters.

PREVENTION

CHILDREN: You must have at least one hero in life, someone that you really look up to because he or she has or represents some excellent qualities or skills that you admire. Maybe you have more than one hero. It could be an older brother or sister, a really good teacher, or an athlete or government leader that you read about in the paper.

Now stop and think for a minute: What is it about that

person or persons that makes you regard them as heroic in your eyes? Grab a paper and pen or pencil and write down the name of each of your heroes, then below their names list those qualities that make you look up to them. Having heroes is great, isn't it? Turn to your parents and tell them about your thoughts on your heroes.

Most of these heroes are people who really are good and care about others. Even if you haven't met them yet, they would probably like you, too, if they met you. But never forget: It is wrong for your hero to ever touch or attempt to touch your private body parts. It is against the law for anyone, even your hero, to treat you in this way. Trusting someone is okay, but not to the point of letting him violate your body by touching or attempting to touch your private parts—those parts covered by your bathing suit.

TIP: If an adult or another child—even one you admire as a hero—touches or attempts to touch your private body parts, demand that person stop! Then tell a parent or other trusted adult.

PARENTS: If your child actually has the opportunity to spend time with a local or national celebrity, such occasion should be chaperoned.

· ·

PRACTICE SCENARIOS

Meghann just adores her English teacher. He is the best teacher she's ever had. On the last day of school, he tells her she has been a great student and he gives her a big hug. What should Meghann do?
If Meghann feels like it, she should hug him back and tell him to have a great summer.

Kevin runs into a well-known local radio personality on the street. When Kevin expresses interest in radio, the deejay offers him a tour of the station if Kevin goes with him right then. What should Kevin do?

Kevin should explain he must get permission first. He should ask the deejay when a convenient time to come to the station would be. Depending on his age, Kevin might want to bring a parent along for the tour.

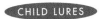

Always check with parents before accepting any chore or job.

The Job Lure

9

While performing various odd jobs, John Wayne Gacy approached young men to ask if they were interested in working with him. Interviews were arranged at his home. Youngsters who brought parents along were told the position had already been filled; then he bid them farewell. Young men who came alone were handcuffed, tortured, and murdered. Thirty-three young men met the same tragic fate at Gacy's hands.

Allowing children, especially older children, to accept jobs or perform chores is a good way for them to learn responsibility, gain independence, and make money. But the offer of a job or short-term errand could be a ruse to abuse or abduct a child. Young children might be offered money on the spot to perform a quick, simple task. Adolescents—and even college students—are nearly always in the market for extra income, and promises of high pay or interesting work are attractive. Perpetrators might post a phony ad or flyer, then schedule interviews with interested youngsters in a secluded location. Baby-sitting jobs accepted through newspaper ads or bulletin boards can also be risky.

Newspaper carriers, Girl Scouts, and other door-to-door solicitors are vulnerable when they visit customers or enter homes unaccompanied. A twelve-year-old New York girl confided to her parents and the newspaper about a "weird" man on her paper route. While collecting money due from customers, Cheri was forced into this man's home. Her instincts had been accurate; Cheri's body was discovered in his basement twenty-four hours later.

• •

PREVENTION

CHILDREN: Just like you, most children have household

chores and errands they are expected to do. What chores do you do around your home? Which do you like most? Which chores do you like least?

You can take pride in doing your chores well, and it makes your parents proud of you. Your family members depend on you to do your share, which is why you are an important part of your family team.

There might also be times that you will be offered small jobs outside the house, such as helping a neighbor with groceries, mowing the grass, or shoveling snow. Before accepting this kind of work, always ask your parents for permission. It is probably okay, but still, ask your parents to be sure.

Keep in mind that there are some people who will lie to you and try to lure you into a dangerous situation with the offer of a job. Just be careful. Of course, you do not need to be afraid of every person who

ever asks you to perform an errand or a small job.

TIP: Always check with your parents before accepting any errand or job. If you are offered a baby-sitting job, don't accept it until your parents have a chance to meet the family for whom you will be sitting. Be sure your parents have the phone number and address. Let your parents know when to expect you home, and call them if you will be late. If you deliver newspapers or sell candy, cookies, or other items door to door, make it a rule never to enter a customer's house unless you are with a trusted grown-up.

PARENTS: Try to accompany youngsters to job interviews, and always double-check pertinent information about any job accepted—employer, location, and hours. The safest jobs are with known and established businesses; young people should not apply for jobs advertised with only a post office box, or appear for interviews in motel rooms or other isolated locations.

For first-time baby-sitting jobs, escort your child to meet the family and inspect the home environment. Be certain you are supplied a phone number. If your instincts tell you the situation is not safe, don't hesitate to stay with your youngster or decline the baby-sitting job altogether. Have your child check in with you periodically, especially if he might be home late. Consider chaperoning your child on his newspaper route, especially before light or after dark. Over the years, a significant number of children have been abducted or molested delivering newspapers.

In the early-morning hours of August 14, 1986, thirteen-year-old Johnny Gosch left home with his dog to deliver a wagonload of newspapers. When the dog returned to Johnny's suburban Des Moines home without him, his parents became alarmed and went searching for him. The wagon, still full of newspapers, was found abandoned. Johnny had disappeared without a trace. He has never been found.

Keep in mind, however, most jobs are legitimate. Knowing that job offers might be used as lures should put most young job-seekers on the alert.

PRACTICE SCENARIOS

Laticia is offered three dollars to watch her neighbor's two young children while their mother goes to the store. What should Laticia do?
Laticia should ask her parents for permission to watch the neighbor's children. If her parents don't know the neighbor, they should meet her first.

Ron is offered a job doing chores around the house of an elderly gentleman. The man promises to pay Ron well, but tells him not to tell his parents about the job. What should Ron do?
Ron should not accept the job. Then he should tell his parents about the secret offer.

Even a total stranger can find out your name.

The Name Recognition Lure 10

By combining the Name Recognition Lure with two other lures, serial killer Ted Bundy effortlessly abducted Kimberly Leach from her Florida school grounds. Bundy, wearing a name tag reading "Richard Burton, Fire Department," called to twelve-year-old Kim by name. (She was wearing a sweatshirt with her name emblazoned on the back.) According to witnesses, Kim began to talk with Bundy, became very distraught, and left with him in a van. Ted Bundy was ultimately executed for the murder of Kimberly Leach.

Well-meaning parents often mark clothes, sports equipment, lunch boxes, and other belongings with conspicuous name tags. This enables potential sex offenders to call the child by name, putting the child off-guard and creating a false sense of trust. A child's name might also be overheard, revealed by another unsuspecting child, or disclosed during casual conversation.

The Name Recognition Lure is often used in conjunction with at least one other lure, such as the Emergency Lure. Example: "Susan, hurry and come with me! Your house is on fire!"

Just prior to Bundy's execution, I attempted to obtain an interview with him. I was very curious to know how he had lured Kim to her death. Although my efforts were in vain, I was able to interview State's Attorney Gerald Blair and his assistant, Robert Dekle, the two attorneys who had prosecuted Bundy. "You're the first person to ask how he did it," I was told. Bundy's lethal combination included:

- The Authority Lure: Bundy wore a name tag that read: "HELLO, My Name Is: Richard Burton, Fire Department."
- The Name Recognition Lure:

Bundy spotted "Kim" on her sweatshirt, then called her by name.

- The Emergency Lure: Bundy later revealed he told Kimberly her house was on fire.

When used in combination, the effectiveness of lures increases significantly.

. . . .

PREVENTION

CHILDREN: When you were born, your parents probably took a lot of care in choosing a name for you. They wanted one that was meaningful. Ask your parents how they picked your name. How do you feel about it? Do you like your name?

People who know you call you by name. There might be times when someone you don't know calls you by your first name. When that happens, it might make you feel important at first, but it can also be confusing. You might wonder, How does this person know my name?

Even a total stranger can find out your name. He might overhear one of your friends calling it out loud. Or he might read it on a sweatshirt or baseball cap you are wearing. Lots of kids put name tags on clothes, sports equipment, musical instrument cases, lunchboxes, and backpacks. If someone can see or read your name tag, then they can pretend to know you. Think about the things you own that need to be labeled. Talk to your parents about how you can safely label them. You might just use your initials or a number code. Or maybe put your name where no one can see it right off.

TIP: If you need to label belongings, put your name where it can't be easily seen.

Why would someone like a stranger take the time to find out your name? It is because they want to make you think you know them. Be careful. People like that might actually be trying to lure you into a dangerous situation.

TIP: Don't trust or go with someone just because they know your name. Listen to that personal siren of yours at times like this!

PARENTS: Stress to your child that under no circumstances should she go with someone simply because the individual knows her name. If your child thinks she doesn't know someone, she probably doesn't.

Review which of your child's possessions need to be labeled. Discuss how you might label these items without endangering her by placing a name tag where it is not visible, or using initials or a number code. Don't allow your child to wear clothing or jewelry broadcasting her name.

. . . .

PRACTICE SCENARIOS

Patrick is playing Frisbee with a group of friends at the park. He is wearing a T-shirt with "Patrick" written across the back. A man approaches him and says, "Patrick! Hey, you probably don't remember me— you were so small the last time I saw you. I'm David Frank. I used to work with your dad. Look, I'm heading over there now to see him, but I'm not sure about the address. Would you like to come along and show me the way?" What should Patrick do?

Patrick should not go with the man under any circumstances. He should tell the man he is not allowed to go anywhere with someone he doesn't know, and even if the man knows his father, Patrick doesn't know him.

Felicia has a new baseball glove and wants to put her name on it so it doesn't get stolen or mixed up with someone else's. What should Felicia do?

Felicia could mark the glove with her initials, use a code or symbol to mark the glove, or write her name on the inside of the glove where it can't be seen.

Make sure your parents always know where you are
and who you are with.

The Playmate/Companion Lure 11

A Houston man lured a little girl into his home with the promise of a coloring book and crayons—the coloring book was X-rated. Over time, he convinced her to reenact some of the pornographic scenes she colored in the book. In short order, he persuaded her to bring along friends. He molested nine of them.

In some instances, child molesters encourage or coerce their victims to usher unsuspecting children into an abusive setting. Once an abuser has manipulated a child with the Playmate Lure, he can make use of one or several other lures—including Affection, Bribery, Fun and Games, Pornography, or Drugs—to initiate sexual contact.

The child molester might make the setting for abuse enticing by creating a party ambiance, plying youngsters with toys or favorite foods. He might project an "anything goes" attitude that can be particularly attractive to adolescents. He depends on word-of-mouth to ensure regular access to children.

Children molested by other children make up the fastest-growing category of sex-crime victims. Twenty percent of sex offenders are children molesting other children. In most cases, the child offender is himself a casualty of abuse and might have no idea his behavior is wrong.

• •

PREVENTION

CHILDREN: You probably have friends you like to play with at recess, after school, and on weekends. What do you like to do with your friends? Do you like to play games, do artwork, watch television, read books, or play computer games? Isn't it nice to have friends? They are an important part of life.

When you make a new friend, it's a good idea to bring them home so your mom and dad can meet them. Your parents will probably want to meet their parents, too. Maybe you can all do something together, like have pizza, go bowling, or watch television.

It's a lot of fun to go places with friends. You might go to the park, to your friend's home, or even to another friend's home. But remember, no matter who you are playing with or where you are playing, no one has the right to touch the private parts of your body or force you to touch his. You already know it's against the law for an adult to do this. Should anyone ever try, tell him to stop. Then leave and tell your parents or another trusted adult.

TIP: Make sure your parents always know where you are and who you are with.

They need to know this to help keep you safe.

PARENTS: Make the effort to know your child's friends and their families. If possible, visit their homes and assess the environment. Strive to make your own home a place children will be eager to visit. Provide youngsters with "supervised freedom" and offer suggestions for projects and games to discourage boredom.

If your child spends time at the house of another playmate, particularly where there is a single male or live-in boyfriend, investigate why that location is so popular. Perform "spot checks" by visiting unannounced during playtime. By the same token, if a child shows a sudden fear of a once-favorite play spot, find out why.

PRACTICE SCENARIOS

Sandra's friend invites her to a secret place to play. It's a house where a man lives alone and will let them do

*If an adult or older kid tries to show you X-rated videos or maga-
zines, you need to tell your parents.*

The Pornography Lure

12

A New York City Police Department employee was arrested for the sexual assault of several minors. His lure: inviting young children to his home to watch Saturday morning cartoons. He alternated regular cartoons with pornographic interpretations of Hansel and Gretel, Snow White, *and other popular childhood stories. Once children became desensitized to the nudity and sex scenes, he persuaded youngsters to imitate what they had seen.*

Many child molesters routinely expose intended victims to pornography in an attempt to convince them that sex between adults and children is normal. Since all children are extremely curious about sex, it is not difficult to hold their interest. Regular exposure to these materials eventually desensitizes youngsters and leaves them vulnerable to abuse. Pornographic magazines and videos are used to stimulate older children, making them easier to seduce.

Children as young as three or four have been known to innocently imitate sexual acts they have seen in pornographic videos or magazines. Exposure to X-rated materials has been linked to many cases where children assault other children.

In February 1993 in Batavia, Ohio, two boys, ages seven and twelve, molested three younger boys while watching their parents' pornographic videos. A local paper quoted the sheriff as saying the boys were motivated to commit the sexual offenses after watching the videos over a period of six months.

Pedophiles might also try to convince youngsters to participate in the production of pornographic photography or videos. Sometimes, this homemade child pornography is then swapped or sold to other pedophiles via word-of-mouth, or even computer bulletin boards. Once a child becomes involved in such an enterprise, the product can be a very effective means of blackmail.

. . . .

PREVENTION

PARENTS: Make a commitment to discuss basic sex education with your child at an early age. As I mentioned earlier, I use bathing suit boundaries to explain "private parts." Although it might be uncomfortable at first, try to create an atmosphere where your child feels free to come to you with any questions about sex. Remember, your child knows what is under a bathing suit and so do you. Keep in mind the molester who told me, "Give me a kid who knows nothing about sex, and you've given me my next victim."

CHILDREN: By this time in your life, your parents may have talked to you about "the birds and the bees": sex education. This might have been un-

comfortable for you, but that is okay. Many people are embarrassed to talk about sex, because it is such a private thing. Your parents might even be a little uncomfortable talking to you about it. But learning about sex is an important part of growing up. You need to understand it.

Do you know what pornography is? Pornography is pictures of naked people in X-rated magazines and videos. Some child molesters show children pornography. Then, they try to talk kids into doing what they saw in the videos or magazines. This is against the law. You now know that the private parts of your body are your own personal property. No grown-up or even an older kid should touch them or ask you to touch theirs.

TIP: If any adult or older kid tries to show you X-rated magazines or videos, you need to tell your parents.

Some child molesters take X-rated pictures or videos of children. Do you know what could happen if someone took those kinds of pictures of you? That person could threaten to show or give them to someone else, unless you do what he says.

TIP: Do not allow anyone to take photographs or videos of you with your clothes off. If someone tries, tell him you don't want to. Then leave and tell your parents or another trusted adult what happened.

PARENTS: Urge your child to tell you immediately about attempts by adults or older kids to show him pornographic materials or take pictures or videos of him without clothing. If your child tells you he has seen X-rated materials, find out where he had access to them and then go to the source.

If your child is acting out sexually, find out how, where, and from whom he learned this behavior. Again, tell him that it is against the law for adults to touch the private parts of his body or force him to touch theirs.

....

PRACTICE SCENARIOS

Tara is watching television one day after school while her mother is at work. Her mother's boyfriend says he has a movie he really wants her to see. But once the video starts to play, Tara realizes that it's X-rated. What should Tara do?
Tara should tell her mother's boyfriend she doesn't want to watch the movie, then tell her mother what happened.

Martha is watching her soap opera while her friend, Theresa, reads. Martha's brother shows Theresa an X-rated magazine and asks if she'd like to read it with him in his room. What should Theresa do?
Theresa should say "No," tell his parents, then report the incident to her own parents.

*If someone threatens you, always tell your parents or a trusted
adult. Threats are against the law.*

Threats and Weapons

13

A Kansas City twelve-year-old girl was walking to school one day when a gunman pulled her into an alley. The girl's screams attracted the attention of a woman on the sidewalk, who hurried to see what was wrong. Upon seeing the woman, the gunman dropped the girl and fled. The twelve-year-old was unharmed.

A child molester or abductor might threaten a child with bodily harm or even death. The mere size of a menacing adult can be intimidating enough to frighten a child into compliance. To keep a victim silent after abuse, a molester plays on a child's greatest fears. Children might be threatened with repercussions if they report abuse, including harm to their loved ones.

■ "If you tell, no one will believe you."

■ "If you tell, your parents won't love you anymore."

■ "If you tell, you'll be sent to jail."

■ "If you tell, I'll hurt you/your parents/your pet."

When frightened, many children choose to remain silent. Confrontation with an actual weapon is rare, but by far the most intimidating means of control. When faced with a gun or knife, most children are understandably frightened into silence and cooperation.

. . . .

PREVENTION

CHILDREN: I want to tell you something before you learn about the Threats and Weapons Lure. Even though this is the scariest lure, you should know that weapons are hardly ever used by child molesters. Most of the time, people try to trick you, but sometimes, threats and weapons are used.

Do you know what a threat is? A threat is when someone says they are going to do something to hurt you or someone you love. Child molesters might use threats to make you go with them, make you do something you don't want to do, or scare you into keeping a secret from your parents.

Keeping a threat secret is a big mistake. For one thing, threats are against the law. For another thing, you should never be afraid to tell a trusted grown-up if you have been threatened. Even if the molester tells you things like, "If you tell, you will get in trouble," or "If you tell, your parents won't love you anymore." Remember, the molester has broken the law, so he will say anything to keep you from telling on him. Your parents can and will help you.

TIP: If someone threatens you, always tell your parents or a trusted adult.

What is a weapon? Some weapons I can think of are guns, knives, and fists. Like threats, weapons can be used to scare people into doing things. If someone were ever to pull a weapon on you, how would you feel? Probably scared, right? The best thing to do if someone threatens you with a weapon is to scream and holler! Keep your head. Run away fast. People who make threats against you don't like it when you start making a lot of noise. They don't want someone else to see or hear what they are trying to do to you.

TIP: If someone ever uses a weapon to try and get you to go with them, run and scream as loud as you can.

PARENTS: Assure your child that nothing she could ever do would make you stop loving her. Let her know that her safety and happiness are your first priority; you will do anything to ensure her well-being.

When faced with a weapon, the child who is paralyzed by fear or follows the perpetrator into a car, building, or isolated area has lost control of the situation. Assure your child that in such cases, weapons are intended to intimidate, but are rarely ever used. Of the molesters I interviewed who used weapons, most told me a loud, attention-getting child is reason to abandon the abduction.

• •

PRACTICE SCENARIOS

Jason is biking home from the store when a woman with a knife tells him to get in her car quietly. What should Jason do?
Jason should do everything he can to call attention to himself and the knife—scream at the top of his lungs. And try to get away.

Whenever Mia's cousin comes to visit, he molests her. Each time, he tells her that if she tells her parents, he will hurt her even worse. Besides, he says, no one will believe her anyway. What should Mia do?
Mia should tell her parents immediately. Her cousin is breaking the law, and he must be stopped from hurting her ever again.

Kids who don't use drugs or alcohol are safer—and smarter—
than kids who do.

The Drug Lure

14

A fifty-three-year-old Monrovia, California, man lured neighborhood boys into his home with alcohol and X-rated videos. The boys, ages ten to thirteen, were then manipulated into having sex.

Child molesters regularly use drugs, especially alcohol, to incapacitate or seduce their victims. Very young children might be tricked into intoxication; older children might willingly experiment with alcohol and other drugs. It's a sad reflection on our country that even elementary students are conceivable prey for the lure of drugs. The Drug Lure is often used in conjunction with pornography to hasten seduction.

Statistics indicate that children under the influence of drugs, especially alcohol, put themselves at much greater risk of sexual assault, either at the hands of an adult molester or even one of their peers.

This is yet another reason to encourage your child to remain drug-free.

The following red flags of concern could indicate your child is using drugs:

- Marked changes in your child's personality, appearance, appetite, and sleeping habits
- Your child's "decent" friends drift away.
- Sudden disinterest in activities and people once important to your child
- School marks suffer.
- Your child displays sudden explicit knowledge of drugs and becomes defensive of drug culture.
- Your child displays unusual distrust or hostility toward you.
- Family valuables and cash begin to disappear.

If you think your child is using drugs, act immediately. Confront her and, if necessary, get professional help.

· ·

PREVENTION

CHILDREN: By now, you have probably heard about drugs. Maybe you even know someone who uses illegal drugs, like marijuana and cocaine. If it hasn't already happened to you, there might be a time when someone comes up to you—probably in secret—to ask you to try drugs. They will pretend to be your friend. They are not. No way.

Maybe you have friends who have already tried drugs and have asked you to join them. Don't. They will try to convince you to take drugs so that you can feel like a "part of the group." That's called "peer pressure." If you are a strong person who cares about your mind and body, you will turn them down. You are to be congratulated for that. Good job!

Drugs can destroy your mind and body. There is nothing good about drugs. In fact, there are many dangers. Using drugs—even just one time—can make you sick, mess up your thinking, take away your skill to be good at things you like, or even kill you. Are drugs worth it? Of course not.

TIP: Stay away from drugs. Don't touch them, no matter what some foolish person tries to tell you. It's better to lose that kind of "friend" than to lose your health—or your life.

PARENTS: Children learn by example, so promote the natural "highs" in life. Be aware of your own drug and alcohol use. Encourage your child to participate in extracurricular activities, since children with many interests are far less likely to experiment with alcohol and other drugs.

CHILDREN: Do you think you would be able to think clearly if you drank alcohol or took other drugs? Would you be more or less able to protect yourself against someone trying to hurt you? Probably less able. Many times, child molesters try to force or talk kids into drinking alcohol or taking drugs. That way, it is easier to abuse them. This is another good reason to say "No" to drugs.

What should you do if an adult or older student tries to get you to take drugs or drink alcohol? Say "No," leave immediately, and tell a trusted adult.

Kids who don't use drugs are safer—and smarter—than kids who do use drugs. Get involved in school and community activities, not drugs.

PRACTICE SCENARIOS

A high school student in Patty's neighborhood wants her to try some pills. The student says the pills will make her feel really good, and people will think she is cool for trying them. What should Patty do?
Patty should say "No, thanks" to the student, and tell a trusted adult about the pills.

The football coach invites Bill over to his house to watch a video of football plays. While Bill is there, the coach encourages him to drink beer. What should Bill do?
Bill should decline the beer, leave the coach's house, and report the incident to his parents—and the school. Adults who encourage young people to drink or take drugs should set off a child's personal siren.

It can be dangerous to go alone to meet someone you know only from on-line.

The Computer/On-Line Lure 15

ichael Austin of Middlesex County, Massachusetts, was sentenced to twenty years for two counts of rape. The thirty-four-year-old man befriended boys during the course of frequent on-line chat sessions. The boys were eventually coaxed into face-to-face meetings where the rapes occurred.

Some child molesters are logging onto the information superhighway to find victims. Using Internet or on-line services, pedophiles can befriend youngsters and, in some cases, lure them into real-life abuse. The anonymous nature of on-line relationships allows users to misrepresent their age, sex, occupation, interests, everything. Unseen, one can create an entirely false identity.

The on-line molester becomes a serious threat if he succeeds in arranging a private, in-person meeting with a youngster. This might be done by using any one of the other lures already discussed. For example:

- **Affection:** He is a good listener who has talked the child through some problems, then suggests they meet in person.
- **Bribery:** He offers free or inexpensive computer hardware or software.
- **Games:** He proposes getting together to play computer or other games.
- **Drugs:** He extends an invitation to a keg party.

You get the idea. Any of the lures in this book could easily appear on-line. Even adults are vulnerable to on-line deception and manipulation.

The on-line pedophile might exploit a youngster's curiosity about sex by introducing sexually explicit dialogue or images into on-line conversation or E-mail.

More than a thousand computer bulletin board services (BBS)

offer pornography in the U.S. One BBS offered over twenty-five thousand X-rated images—six thousand included children.

. . . .

PREVENTION

PARENTS: Do your homework. Bring yourself up to speed on the information superhighway, especially if your child is already riding it. Explore its positive features and educational advantages with him.

CHILDREN: Many young people just like you are getting a chance to work, play, and explore on computers. Some of you use them at school and some kids even have one at home. They can be a lot of fun and are a great learning tool.

If you use computers, you probably know about on-line access. It lets you talk with people all over the world! Most on-line users are just like you—friendly people trying to make new friends. That is good, but you still need to be very careful. You wouldn't tell a stranger on the street things about yourself, so why would you do it on the computer? It just doesn't make sense.

TIP: Do not give out your full name, address, or phone number.

You might meet someone on-line who wants to meet you in person. If you want to meet them, don't go alone. An adult should go with you. Since you can't see or hear the people on-line, they can pretend to be someone they are not. They could be dangerous.

TIP: It can be dangerous to go alone to meet someone you know only from on-line, because the person might not be who he says he is.

PARENTS: The time your child spends on-line is deserving of the same scrutiny as time spent watching television and films. Make an effort to know where your child is spending his time on-line and supervise him if necessary.

CHILDREN: When someone sends you letters, pictures, or stories it's called "E-mail." Child molesters sometimes send X-rated E-mail to kids on-line. In the Pornography Lure chapter, you learned how molesters use pornography to lure children. If you receive any X-rated E-mail, show it to your parents immediately. It could be from a molester.

PARENTS: Urge your child to tell you about any unsolicited E-mail which is threatening or sexually explicit. Most on-line services have parental control features which allow you to limit your child's access to different areas of the system, usually those devoted to chatting or the exchange of sexually explicit images or conversation. Just as there are places inappropriate for children in real space, so are there such places in cyberspace.

PRACTICE SCENARIOS

Valerie is chatting with some people on-line. Suddenly, someone with the screen name "XXXman" sends her assorted X-rated pictures and stories. What should Valerie do?
Valerie should show the mail to an adult immediately. Valerie and the adult should then report "XXXman" to the on-line service and the police.

Joshua spends a lot of time on-line lately, chatting with his new friend, "Eric655321." They seem to have a lot in common and, as it turns out, they live in the same city. One day, "Eric655321" proposes they meet. What should Joshua do?
If Joshua really wants to meet his on-line friend, he should take a parent with him for the first meeting. Remember, since you can't see or hear on-line friends, it is possible for them to make up anything about themselves.

Appendix

What to do if Sexual Abuse Occurs

Should you discover your child has been sexually abused, I suggest the following course of action:

- Offer love and support. Encourage your child to talk openly about what happened: where, when, and with whom.
- Try to keep your own emotions under control so as not to scare your child.
- Stress that it is not the child's fault—the child is a victim, the abuser is a criminal.
- Report the abuse to police immediately.
- Contact your family physician. It is important that a child be examined by a physician as soon as abuse is disclosed.
- Obtain counseling for your child.

If Your Child is Missing

It is important to know who your child's friends are, their phone numbers, and where they live. Be familiar with your child's routines and the places he frequents. If you can not locate your child:

- Don't panic.
- Search your house and grounds thoroughly. (Your child might just be asleep somewhere close by.)
- Call your child's friends to determine if they know his/her whereabouts.
- Search your child's usual "hangouts."

If you are still unable to locate your child, the next step is to determine which missing child category your youngster falls into.

Categories of Missing Children

There are four recognized categories of missing children: Runaways, Throwaways, Parental Abductions, and Criminal Abductions.

- **Runaways:** voluntary departure by the child
- **Throwaways:** involuntary departure of the child at the demand of parents
- **Parental Abduction:** abduction of the child by a parent, usually as a result of a custody dispute during separation/divorce/abuse allegations
- **Criminal Abduction:** abduction of the child by a person who does not have permanent or temporary guardianship of the child, usually someone unknown to the child

While all four categories are potentially dangerous, criminal abduction poses the greatest immediate threat to life and limb. Forensic pathologists estimate the average life expectancy of a criminally abducted child to be fourteen to forty-eight hours. Therefore, it is imperative to determine as quickly as possible the status of your missing child. Ask yourself:

- Are there unhappy circumstances within the home (pending/recent divorce, sexual abuse, physical violence, alcoholism)?
- Has the child recently been depressed, withdrawn, or moody?
- Has the child lost enthusiasm for activities once important to him?
- Have the child's grades dropped recently?
- Has the child suddenly withdrawn from favorite family members or friends?
- Has the child acquired new friends of whom you disapprove?
- Does the child have a history of substance use/abuse?
- Has the child ever run away (or threatened to) from home?
- Are any of the child's clothes missing?
- In cold weather, is the child's coat missing?
- Is money missing?

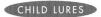

■ Are any of the child's favorite possessions (dolls, diary, photos, music cassettes/CDs, etc.) missing?

If the answer to most of these questions is *yes*, your child is likely a runaway. Contact your local police department. Keep in mind that most runaways return within three days. Contact your child's friends and put out the word that your child is welcome home. Most children who run away discuss the prospect with friends first, and might even count on them for a place to stay.

If the answer to most of these questions is *no, call the police immediately*. Review the criteria with them. Explain why you believe your child has been criminally abducted.

Be prepared to give:
■ a recent photograph
■ physical description
■ description of clothing worn when last seen
■ description of any special identifying marks
■ where child was last seen/was going to/was coming from

Don't rely entirely on the police—time is of the essence.
■ Mobilize relatives, neighbors, your child's friends and their families, clergy.
■ Ask everyone to immediately contact their VIP community contacts (police chief, district attorney, district representative, mayor).
■ Go door to door. There is nearly always someone who has seen something.
■ Notify the media. (Research these phone numbers in your local Yellow Pages.)
  ■ Television—assignment editor/producer
  ■ Radio stations—station manager
  ■ Newspaper—city desk editor

Provide the media with all relevant information (such as physical description, approximate time and location) and urge immediate action.

- Post someone on the home telephone.
- Keep a line open at all times. (If needed, contact the phone company for emergency call-waiting.)
- Incoming calls must be pertinent and very brief.
- Stress the fourteen- to forty-eight-hour life expectancy of the criminally abducted.
- Urge police and media cooperation.

NOTE: The above action should be taken only when you have determined your child is in danger. Mobilizing an entire community could result in costly financial obligations. For the sake of all involved, don't "cry wolf."

Final Thoughts

arenthood is a supreme human experience. It endows us with instinctive personal wisdom—the signals or hunches we receive from the pit of our stomachs. No one is perfect, though, and in the long process of rearing children we all make some poor decisions (usually when we fail to listen to our parental intuition). And yes, some parents probably don't deserve to be parents. However, the vast majority of us are hard-working and caring people. We don't give up. We will go on doing what our hearts tell us is best for our children.

We are often challenged by the media. It seems as if every time the media reports a social problem, we are bombarded with soundbite opinions of "experts" declaring the breakdown of the American family. The modern family, especially the nontraditional family, is increasingly becoming a convenient whipping boy, taking the blame for a growing number of social and political ills. While I am not blind to the storms that batter modern-day families—divorce, unemployment, infidelity, crime, substance abuse, teen pregnancy, etc.—nor am I blind to the unheralded and untiring efforts of those family members who, despite the hardest of times, hold their families together. While it is the media's job to magnify and examine problems, their running obituary for the American family can take its toll on parental confidence. Such negative and inaccurate views often succeed in making us forget the timeless inner strength of the family.

Like a lone sentinel standing guard, history has seen the passing of powerful monarchs, dictators, and presidents as the family continues to march forward. Wars are fought, civilizations and nations rise and fall as the family marches forward. In personal diaries, letters, photographs, and the arts, history has faithfully recorded that not even the evils of slavery, genocide, war, and their aftermath can completely sever the physical and emotional bonds of the family unit. The family marches onward.

After the first atomic bomb exploded over Hiroshima, Japan, in 1945, every social institution was destroyed save one: the family. Within the city, parents and grandparents searched through deadly debris for loved ones. Brothers and sisters, many badly burned, most frightened beyond words, searched the hellish landscape determinedly for their siblings. While every other institution—military, governmental, religious, and educational, disappeared, the family endured; all within a vacuum of horror never before known to the world. The family marched onward.

On Mexico's Yucatan Peninsula, on the outskirts of the famous ruins of Chichen Itza, I have seen Mayan Indian families carrying out daily chores around their grass-roofed dwellings. They were cooking, providing heat and shelter for themselves and their young. Their language and culture were foreign to me, but a Mayan mother's quick glance and gentle reprimand towards her child needed no translation. It is a universal language; the language of parental concern. There, under the shadows of ancient ruins, the Mayan family marches onward.

As parents, each of us understands the instinct to protect and care for our children. Our caring actions demonstrate an abiding love. We get up each day and work to make a better life for those we brought into this world. With each passing generation, that same loving concern is rekindled and passed on within the family. The family can persevere through any hardship, endure any tragedy, because love is forever.

Please take heart in the knowledge that, for the most part, we're doing an excellent job as parents. According to the 1993 Gallup Youth Survey, "America's Youth in the 1990s":

- 94 percent of American youth state that they are happy.
- 93 percent are excited about the future.
- 90 percent feel very close to their families.
- 88 percent say that they are likely to marry.
- 84 percent want to have children.
- 86 percent are satisfied with their personal lives.
- 78 percent desire to reach the top of their chosen careers.

Mom and Dad, we must be doing something right because these numbers are significant. They are testament to your work, sacrifice, and love. We have reason to be proud! Take heart and do not be discouraged by constant, negative reports that the family is in decline or worse. Remember, you and your family make up the core of this country and our vast world. It is you who labor in the work force stimulating our economic growth. It is you who shoulder the burden of government to function with hard-earned tax dollars. It is you who supply the military with sons and daughters to protect our freedom and way of life. Even organized religion could barely survive without you. Your charity knows no bounds.

As parents, you are deserving of respect and appreciation for a difficult job well done. The fact that you've made this book a part of your family's library speaks to your commitment to responsible parenting. Hopefully, one day, your child will pass this information on to your grandchildren, remembering your love and concern. It is my fondest hope that in some small way this book and its message helps to strengthen and protect that unique bond between you and your loved ones. It is a gift from my family to yours.